the awakening dream

journey on the wings of a thousand angels

by: p.d.jacob

THE AWAKENING DREAM

Journey on the Wings of a Thousand Angels

Published by Lulu

Photos by Paul D. Jacob

Cover photo by Jefras (jefras@netmadeira.com)

ISBN 978-1-4357-4409-7

Dedication

If you live in the Fox Valley region of Wisconsin, U.S.A., you may be familiar with a nonprofit coffeehouse called Harmony Café. I call it a coffeehouse but it is so much more. The Harmony Café welcomes grandparents and grandkids and everyone in between. Diverse races and lifestyles merge for an eclectic mix of social events, entertainment and life-skills programming. All of this occurs under the nurturing umbrella of many community-minded individuals and organizations. Goodwill Industries of North Central Wisconsin has been a pioneering force behind the great things happening here. But it is the collective consciousness that truly drives this unique environment, and solidifies its success.

One of the most remarkable aspects, and one that earned my respect early on, is the Café's focus on youth, particularly youth seeking a bit of support and/or guidance. The kids are also involved with the day-to-day operations of the Café, and help to plan and organize events. These youth give me great inspiration! I have watched many of them evolve from insecure observers to socially conscious community activists. So, I dedicate this book about spirituality to all who have put their spirits into the virtual coffee mug of the Harmony Café. You rock the world! Well, at least this little corner of it!

- p.d.jacob

the breeze

My bedroom window is open just enough to invite a gentle breeze to take a shortcut through the house. I lay on the bed with no covers, soothed by the air flow, one thousand heavenly angels gently massaging my body. The hustle and bustle of the world have been left behind as I drift slowly toward my dream world. I imagine my fingers, toes, legs and arms are becoming invisible. They disappear and fall away from my body and from my mind. Now the angels who caress me have my fullest attention. They whisper softly as they flow over my ear, enticing me to join them on tonight's holy pilgrimage. With sweet kisses they promise that this night's journey will enrich my spirit, and will provide me with a more personal connection to the butterflies of the meadow and the trees of the forest. My angels speak of total harmony and integration. They talk of love and compassion and teaching and learning. They point beyond the horizon in all directions, saying; "The bounty of the universe is everywhere, even right here where you sleep." They smile with a confident wisdom that gains my trust and peaks my interest. I let go. And I embark with little resistance.

As my consciousness slowly rises, my body remains. It will wait patiently, and so shall the world I am so familiar with, until my return. But for now my spirit must be free and unencumbered as it merges with the choir of angels who ride the breeze. My essence quickly gains momentum as if I have been tossed into a stream. There is no fear as my familiar surroundings shrink and disappear in the distance

behind me. There is only anticipation and wonder about what lies ahead as the breeze carries me away.

Floating, floating like a feather I am weightless. There are no laws of physics here. In my dream I am massless, yet my contemplation is evidence that I truly do exist. In the company of angels I have 'become' the breeze. I can swoop up and down, and tickle the leaves on the tree branches. I can soar and spin and make dust rise up and dance. I can push sails, and coax man's best friend to hang his head out of the car window. Then I can make his tongue flutter and send slobber droplets spewing through the air. I can face the dove in flight and make her work twice as hard, or I can chase her tail and double her speed. I can even rest and do nothing if ever I tire. My newfound freedom makes me laugh with joy as I blow across my endless new playground, so much to see, so much to do.

Over the fields of grain I soar, and I delight in brushing the tops of each and every plant. With my gentle touch the fields become a symphony of motion, singing to all who care to look. The tall grasses in the meadow play along, and I am the conductor. I carry their seeds and spores to far away locations, expanding their families and ensuring their survival. In this moment in time, the fields and I are united in movement and purpose. We are appreciatively codependent and intertwined. We move as one.

I continue to experiment, brushing the face of a deer, making her blink three times. With a little more speed, I graze her nose and she shakes her head and snorts. In return for being a party to my amusement, I carry the aroma of ripe apples from a tree across the valley to my new friend. Her white tail flashes as she hops away toward her next meal. I smile, then I move on as well.

The sun warms me. And as a messenger of the sun I spread that warmth across the land and to the faces of sun worshipers. I dry the wings of emerging butterflies to prepare them for their maiden flight. I help to warm the reptile's blood so he can go about his business of the day. Then we all hold hands for a moment, my angels and I, and together we help to evaporate and purify the standing waters so they can fall back to earth as rain, giving continuing life to all below. I take with me this lesson: That as individual notes our purpose here is obscure. But when we combine together in song we are an orderly choir; loud and clear and directed. Life sings in harmony. Harmony is the song of life.

I free-fall for just a moment as I am released by my angels, then soar forward to continue my exploration and play. My mentors are never far away. But they understand that followers will never learn to chart a course, and passengers will never develop the skills of a pilot. So they encourage my innocent rendezvous with fate and patiently wait for lessons to reveal themselves to me along my path. The angels know that all moments are teachable, and that the most difficult are also the most valuable.

I see a little boy playing by a creek and I swing by to say hello in my usual way. I toss his blond hair back and forth over his face and ruffle his baggy t-shirt. He doesn't mind at all. In fact, I think he likes it. I want to see his eyes so I send a little howl through the tops of the pine trees and he looks up for a second or two. His eyes are brown and his eyes are happy. The boy has happy eyes and he's having fun today. That makes me happy too! I make another wisp through the pine branches hoping to steal a parting glance from brown eyes as I sail into the provocative horizon.

introspection

I travel for days and am overwhelmed by the beauty of all that my dream reveals. I'm well aware that my body remains snug in my bed, in my home, in my town. Yet I have never known such exquisite detail or emotional elation even though I've walked many of these places wide-awake. In my sleep, my spirit travels and learns and grows, as the essence of who I am expands to encompass the greater world:

that which I am unable to see with my eyes or describe with my voice. I'm experiencing the world from my pillow just as I have from my desk or my chair when I have found myself lost in a vivid daydream. This can only mean the entire universe is within me somehow, and I within it, just as the angels had whispered; "The bounty of the universe is everywhere, even right here where you sleep." And indeed, the universe yields its treasures to those who don't resist.

I'm suddenly illuminated by the realization that my angels and I aren't sleeping, in the sense that we're unaware of our surroundings. We're fully awake, though in a different part of the world. This part of the world is shielded, except when we allow ourselves to become open-minded, with cleansed imaginations. Where is this place I visit and experience without the use of my five senses?

No artist, whose paintings may fetch millions of dollars at auction, is capable of capturing the multifaceted beauty of a golden sunset, or the essence of an intricately designed dragonfly. No poet, though her pen may play our deepest emotions like gentle fingers on a harp, is capable of opening our eyes to the full rapture of the universe. Just as we can only physically touch objects that are within arm's length, so all of our senses are limited by their physical relationship to the world around us. Some things which make up this vast and dimensional universe are beyond our reach, out of sight, have no sound as our ears know sound, no smell as we know scent, and no taste as our tongues know flavor.

The angels dwell in this special place, just beyond normal comprehension, a place which supports the more familiar world which we 'can' actually see, touch, feel, smell and taste. Some call this mysterious region the collective consciousness. Some call it God. Others refer to it as the harmonious interaction of the universe, or as life energy. And then there are those who believe this dimension is the spirit world, where our souls take up residence after death and before birth: The spirit world, where forces are at work intervening and interfering, suggesting a supernatural essence or being at work here. My angels know that this mysterious place, regardless of what we choose to call it, is both within us and all around us. It is not a part of our consciousness, but rather we are a part of its consciousness. It lives as the ultimate totality. And we are no more than, nor less than, individual cells in the great body of life.

We all step over the threshold from our personal consciousness to the spiritual domain now and then. But our time there is typically brief and fleeting, as our self-imposed obligations drag us out, and back to

our self-imposed reality. Our materialistic desires tend to overpower our spiritual needs, and so we lose touch with our spirituality. We get stuck in our insulated spheres, unwilling or unable to cast off our armor and take a leisurely swim in our deep-seated fantasies. So sad. :-(

In an act of cantankerous defiance, I'm suddenly inspired to test the boundaries of my imagination. I split into a billion, trillion molecules and explode into space, zooming past planets, comets and a superabundance of celestial shapes and particles. Balls of burning gas larger than anything a human mind can imagine litter the vast expanse. Spinning disks of dust, black holes, soaring chunks of ice and solar systems too numerous to count vie to be recognized on an infinite backdrop of darkness.

What I had known as outer space is neither outer nor space. It is directly connected to my mind and my backyard. And it is filled with every element in every combination, in every shape and form. There are stories here, too, hidden amongst the stars which tell of the birth of space and time, and the creation of all things. The stories are encrypted, and we struggle to decipher one sentence at a time. To reveal any more would rob us of the wonder and amazement we feel as we peer through our telescopes and theorize about our very existence.

My molecules speed toward nowhere because there is no outer edge to serve as a destination. That makes time rather inconsequential and meaningless on this cosmic excursion. I slow, and then retreat back to my more familiar surroundings here on earth. I miss the shiny pebbles on the creek bottom. I miss the smell of wet leaves on the forest floor and the sound of children on the playground.

unusual notion

The spiritual dimension is an odd concept, because within our limited sphere of understanding we haven't encountered anything that defies explanation, or at least invokes a good theory to be tested. Everything we are familiar with comes from somewhere, or is the result of something. Everything has a beginning and an end, a front and a back, an origin and a destination. Even the complex laws of physics which determine the movements of planets and subatomic particles continue to yield their secrets. With every new generation of scientists we probe deeper into inner and outer space, and develop more advanced technologies to measure and record the interactions of objects. For example, we know that our solar system is in the Milky Way galaxy, and that the next nearest large galaxy is two million light years away. We know that these two galaxies are expected to collide with catastrophic consequences in about three billion years.

We know that photon particles (light energy) which originate at the core of our sun, travel at the speed of light, 186 thousand miles per second. It takes approximately eight minutes for those photons to travel from the sun to the earth. This means the earth is eight 'light minutes' from the sun. Eight light

minutes is a very long distance, indeed. But, scientists have identified and described objects in the universe that are tens of billions of light 'years' away from planet earth. Is there a clue to life hidden in the fact that the distant galaxies are made of the same elements that make up my pillow, Mount Everest, the deer and the apple tree? My angels say so. They encourage me to be humbled by my small, yet important role in the grand scheme of the living macrocosm.

Back on earth now, and having collected myself together, I flow leisurely over field and glen, stirring the insects and pollen. Green grasshoppers and big brown june bugs whirl right through me, tickling my belly. I inhale the scent of myriad flowers that look up from below, decorating the terrain like a beaded purse. Chemists would be proud of me as I drift down through the gorges and surge over the hilltops, blending the different fragrances into aromatic perfumes. The smells, colors, sounds and textures invigorate everything, just as they have since long before my earliest ancestors made footprints on riverbanks. I catch a tiny feather in my virtual palm and carry it for nearly a mile, then set it gently on a pond where it continues to surf, due east.

My angels and I close our eyes, partly in hopeful prayer, partly in appreciation for what we tend to overlook and take for granted. Imagine having lived for some time on the barren moon, my angels wonder aloud, and then being transported to this living planet. It is a heaven unto itself, filled with wondrous gifts of pleasure and beauty, its inhabitants infinitely diverse and spectacular. It is a priceless bank of treasures for the senses, open to anyone who chooses to turn the key and enter her domain.

Humankind is a newcomer to the universe, and even to planet earth. The amount of time our species has existed represents only a tiny splinter in the timeline of life on earth. Even our individual life spans pale in comparison to other life forms. The five-thousand-year-old Bristlecone Pine trees of the Rocky Mountains are possibly the oldest living things on the planet. Some of these standing trees were seedlings when the great pyramids of Egypt were under construction. If they could speak, what would they say? They do speak, my angels insist, but do we listen?

We have the intelligence to be worthy custodians of our planet's treasures, yet our arrogance has caused us to exploit the earth's resources and drive other life forms to extinction. With knowledge and power comes responsibility. Our vast knowledge of the earth's delicate ecosystem should teach us to respect nature, to recycle our products, to retain pristine wildlife areas, to encourage the development of renewable, green energy sources, and to appreciate the diverse beauty of nature, which is an integral and inseparable part of our own physical and spiritual existence.

dimensions

It is nothing short of a miraculous feat that our species has unlocked so many secrets of the universe. We have accumulated libraries full of facts relating to space and time, and matter and life. All of these incredible facts, however, belong to the dimension accessible by our senses. They do not belong to the dimension where I fly with angels, and where I choose my own laws of physics to suit my dreams and my imagination.

How does this unrevealed kingdom influence the decisions we make and the lives we lead? Its function is indeed to provide that which our soul craves, yet is unable to acquire through our five familiar senses. Without spirituality we are unable to tap the tree of wisdom which enlightens us to our purpose, to our creator if there is one, to how the universe came from nothingness, and to what lies beyond the outer edge. How and when did time 'start', and will time ever 'stop'? Will my mind live on after my body dies? What is my divine relationship to someone who lives on the other side of the planet, whom I've never met, or to someone who has yet to be born? What is my cosmic relationship to a bird, or a flower, or a raindrop? Were the basic elements that miraculously combined to make life once drifting through the universe long before the stars and planets were formed? And if so, was it by 'chance'

that these elements eventually combined to form life? And finally, why do I have a need to seek answers to these questions when it seems other life forms here on earth neither care nor have the ability to ponder such complexities?

This is where science ends and spirituality, religion and faith begin. Or you could say: This is where spirituality, religion and faith 'join' science. My angels know the distinction is irrelevant. They smile in the knowledge that science, spirituality, religion and faith are only four mentionable ingredients in a recipe that requires many more ingredients if it is to satisfy all of our hungers. They also understand that our questions endear us to our universe even more than the answers we seek. The questions provide a fascinating element of wonderment, adding color and awe to the virtual banquet of life.

My angels lure me to the seaside where I spend my

mid day. I rock the waves back and forth, cleansing the shoreline with salt and foam. Beach bums and tanners appreciate my cool breath on such a warm day. Occasionally I treat them to a mist of ocean spray which I snag from the sea on my way in. The sea and I have quickly become good friends. We play together all day without getting tired. I send a Frisbee way over the grasp of an intended recipient. We both laugh as I flow over his head, and toward the seaside town nearby.

The vendors are out peddling their goods. It was the noisy activity of their outdoor marketplace that called me inland from the sand dunes and dried seaweed. I whip around and through tripods, table legs and booths, admiring the human hearts and souls expressed on canvass and in glass figurines. Arts and crafts of every type line the sidewalks, hoping to strike a chord with the next passerby. Pairs of eyes

carefully scan the creations hoping to make a connection between that which is viewed and that which is waiting to be stirred within the viewer.

It is this subliminal, spiritual realm within us that the artist is hoping to reach. The painter's reward is not just in knowing that we paused to take a look at his work, but that his work has 'touched' us somehow. The photographer will be praised when his photo communicates something that cannot be seen. The poet will be truly successful if her verses take us beyond the words on the paper, to a place deep within.

The artist's work is actually greater than the sum of its parts because art is capable of taking us beyond the limits of our five senses. Art is an expression of our spiritual component. Art in any form offers us a fleeting glimpse into that mysterious place; that place which should be visited regularly, because it provides life-giving nourishment for our souls. We see what we were blind to. We hear where we were deaf. We feel where we thought we had no feelings.

Nature, too, is a kindred sister of art. And both dwell in the recesses of our spirituality. How many of us have felt in touch with that spiritual place as we sat alone on a riverbank and watched the water flow, or became mesmerized by the dancing flames of a campfire, or gazed into a star-filled night sky? During these moments we have one foot in that special world. We would do well to push our foot in a bit further, and leave it in a bit longer, my angels gently advise. They are aware of the rejuvenating powers available to our minds, to our souls, to our spirits.

the plight

As we cross the threshold into that mysterious and fascinating spiritual place, we are presented with a monumental dilemma. Because we are limited by our five senses, and caged by the constraints of our written and spoken languages, we have a difficult time describing these abstract notions. In our feeble attempt to describe the indescribable, we've clothed these elusive forces in metaphoric stories. Enter the Greek and Roman gods and goddesses, who were thought to be responsible for everything we experienced: fire, love, light, wine and grain, everything! Since the beginning of recorded history, be it cave wall paintings or stories passed down through the generations, human beings have satisfied their hunger for a sensible solution to life's mysteries by conjuring plausible gods and deities.

My tutors urge me toward the jungles of Central America. I wind my way through the dense foliage under a canopy teaming with activity. Every tree, it seems, is a world of its own, supporting millions of life forms from the microscopic to the jaguar and the howler monkey. Who could separate the animal life from the plant life when the entire forest is alive and moving, and breathing? My angels do not allow me to overlook the fact that even the soil, the sky and I are quintessential components of this enormous organism. When we all join forces, then the breath of life commences.

The jungle is so vast that she is capable of keeping many secrets. Yet one is reluctantly emerging from the vegetation as archeologists invade her abyss.

Great cities and complex civilizations which once flourished in her midst, were long ago consumed by 2,500 species of vines, some 3,000 feet in length and the width of trees.

I drift over the crumbled, stone mounds which once were majestic temples reaching beyond the treetops, bidding to touch the gods. Some structures have survived intact, allowing me to contribute a draft through musty arches, corridors and alcoves. The dwellers who passed through these arches thousands of years ago had a profound sense of the spiritual as well. Sacred symbols, ceremonial altars and descriptive hieroglyphics speak of a culture whose roots were embedded in the pacification and appeasement of 'their' gods. I dare say the human psyche's quest for spiritual fulfillment has not changed much since the feet of these ancient inhabitants strolled the cobblestone walkways to their city square.

Depending directly upon the family each of us happens to be born into, or the culture we happen to be raised in, we might refer to our personal divine entity as Allah, or as God, or the Buffalo, the Cobra, the Sun or the Moon, or any number of worldly objects and beings which were personified to give us something within our grasp of understanding to call our creator and the conductor of life's mysteries. Our brains just insist there's got to be somebody behind the scenes, running the show. I, too, am challenged, struggling to find acceptable words to explain these concepts. So I use phrases like; an invisible dimension, an inner world, beyond the senses. Even my angels have been called spirits and gods and other names by people who have known them as fondly as I do. I believe you know my angels even though I pluck words from the dictionary to

describe them and the realm that embodies them.

If we were able to communicate with one another telepathically, we wouldn't have created such controversy by attempting to describe these intangible notions using words and concepts that just don't fit. But we aren't telepathic. So, like trying to push square pegs into round holes, we use familiar words and ideas to share these concepts and pass our beliefs down to future generations. The problem with our inadequate descriptions became quite evident as civilizations expanded and stories began to clash. Spirituality should conceivably unite the masses, because it seems to be something all of mankind has in common - something we share.

Unfortunately, religion, which some people describe as institutionalized or commercialized spirituality, often divides the masses. The followers of Buddha, Aphrodite, Allah, Jesus Christ and Brahma do not worship in the same house, or build upon their commonalities. Yet each of these divine entities provides a link to the same spiritual world for its followers. Each of these entities is a manifestation of the same angelic zephyr which happens to be my spiritual journey tonight. My angels know that contrary to what is often taught, God has many faces, each intending to be a safe haven, and each smiling upon the other. With sadness, the angels acknowledge that most people do not know God in this way. And, so, would-be friends become foes, and neighbors become enemies.

I zip through a clearing and take out a little of my frustration by scattering organic debris through the air, interrupting the otherwise tranquil surroundings. The butterflies are blown off course and briefly redirected. The ants expeditiously tend to their nests, reopening their doorways. Birds flit and

scatter, but return as quickly as they departed. In a matter of minutes the critters resume their regular routine and the evidence of my tantrum disappears.

There's room for all of us on this tiny planet, my angels profess. And our religions and spiritual intuitions guide us toward the clues to living harmoniously. Clues, not answers, are what we have to work with. The answers will reveal themselves, albeit differently to each of us, as we listen to and trust our instincts, as we incorporate the clues and move forward through life.

We all walk a spiritual path in addition to our career path and educational aspirations. Our spiritual path is a guide of moral conduct, a mixture of beliefs and faith that determine our actions and our interactions with others. And which will also provide a sense of purpose and connection to the world in which we live. Some of us will choose a well-defined path already outlined by the religion we subscribe to. We'll follow the teachings of that religion passed down from an earlier time, and usually through our own family lineage. The religions of the world, and spiritual beliefs of distinct cultures, have played a huge role in teaching morality, compassion and responsibility. They've given countless individuals and entire civilizations purpose and motivation. It's unlikely that civilizations could have developed and flourished without the collective sense of unity and structure provided by a code of moral expectations for its members. After all, what would be the purpose for villages and cities other than to gather closer together for the common good, and to join forces with a common goal or destination in sight. In this sense, organized religion has played an important, if not necessary, role in our personal and societal evolution.

a paradox

On the other hand, misinterpretations of the written and spoken words continue to inspire misguided fools to engage in some of the most inhumane and uncivilized atrocities against humankind. Religions by their very nature are usually incompatible with one another. They are quite matter-of-fact and often have little tolerance for opposing views. My earliest perspective on this subject came from my Christian upbringing. How ironic, I thought, that religion was supposed to provide my moral compass, yet religious intolerance seemed to be responsible for more oppression, persecution and bloodshed than any natural disaster I could think of. My religion had endorsed annihilation, slavery, witch hunts and second-rate status for women and other minorities. The leaders of my country claimed we built 'one nation under God' yet we abducted boatloads of Africans, tearing them from their families and homelands to be bought, sold and enslaved here. During that same period, my religious forefathers were systematically displacing, or murdering, almost the entire Native American population so we could exploit their land and resources. Is this not genocide? It all seemed eerily similar to Adolf Hitler's claim to infamy, though I never read about this correlation in any of my school books.

As I emerge from the jungle, the sweet smell of damp compost fades. I'm able to increase my speed as I hurry toward the open shoreline. The seabirds

are waiting just ahead. They depend on me to lift their silhouettes high into the sky and then hold them against the blueness. A bird's-eye view for the predator, and the unsuspecting prey below shimmer like sequins under the glossy skin of the bay. For an instant I feel a sense of pity for those lower on the food chain. Their unchosen obligation, their sad fate, seems to be self-sacrifice to the larger and more fortunate. But before my journey is complete I will understand that no link in this chain is above or below another. And that every link is dependent on the link to the right and the link to the left. This chain has no beginning and no end. The mighty lion and the great white shark will one day be claimed by the scavengers, insects and bacteria. 'Mighty' is a relative term here, and one that becomes misleading as our understanding deepens and our perspective broadens.

Many of us have struggled to reconcile our need for spirituality with the seemingly inconsistent or contradictory nature of religions. That's why we must question and scrutinize the self-appointed representatives of our religious faith: those who do the teaching. That doesn't necessarily mean we should discount the religions or the teachers. It just means we should examine the teachers' interpretations of the underlying messages at the core of our faith. We need to acknowledge that these teachings were written, translated and passed down by imperfect and subjective men.

It's clear that many religious stories and myths reflect the thoughts and cultures of their time, and that all is not applicable in today's world. Many of us can breathe a sigh of relief knowing we can acceptably ignore some biblical instruction. For example, those who commit adultery and brides who

are not virgins no longer have to fear being stoned to death. And those of us who enjoy our pork, bacon and ham no longer fear the wrath of God. Again, this doesn't mean the underlying principles of religious teachings are invalid, only that the stories and metaphors used to express the concepts may be outdated, and even counterproductive in the twenty-first century.

If instead of interpreting all of these stories literally, we realize that they are attempting to express a thought or prove a point using the words and ideas of that time period, we would surely avoid many conflicts and unresolvable debates. Could it be that a common thread of spiritual truth runs through the fabric of all of the various religions, but that this truth has been distorted by man's feeble attempt to describe that which transcends description? Could it be that the underlying messages have been misinterpreted by the readers, or even the writers, in some cases? Could it be that by cloaking the misunderstood miracles of life in man-made gods and deities, we have diluted and altered pure spirituality which is the core of all things? Historical religious and mythological accounts are heavy with reference to man's inability to comprehend, let alone describe, the essence of spirituality. The concept is elusive, because spirituality is a place where all of us walk, but where none of us live.

We can be frustrated by our inability to fully understand this dimension. Or we can choose to enjoy the wonder of it all. We can feel threatened by other individuals and cultures who've found alternative deities and gods to fill this void. Or we can appreciate and rejoice in our commonality, which seems to drive all of us to explore and connect with that uncharted dimension.

sea to sea

The ocean seems endless as I move steadily on what has become an international voyage. I rest for days in mid-flight when all is calm. Other times I join great storms, and produce water spouts and hurricanes. Those who travel the shipping lanes have great respect for me because they know, if I am so inclined, I can join with the waves to toss even the largest of seagoing vessels. Riding the waves gives me plenty of time to think about all that my angels have revealed to me on this quest for enlightenment. They've given me seeds of thought to cultivate with analysis and synthesis. The flower that grows will feed my spiritual hunger. And as I pull back each petal, I will find more treasures to cultivate and more thoughts to analyze. I will also treasure the fragrance which escapes as I peel each petal away.

The planet confesses how small she actually is as I approach the shore of another continent. People are people wherever I find them; walking, talking, eating, sleeping. They love, and cry, and care for their children the same way in the eastern hemisphere as they do in the west. Before my thought is complete, angel wings gesture through the animal kingdom, exposing the mothers and fathers there, who tenderly care for and protect their young too, not unlike mankind. Father penguin balances the

unhatched egg on his feet for days, protecting it from cold death. Mother water buffalo charges the fierce lion who crept too close to a vulnerable yearling. The marsupials carry their children in their pockets until the youngsters are mature enough to venture out on their own. And the children? They run and play and laugh in any language, with a curious innocence that prepares and trains them for what's to come as days and years draw them forward.

Having shown the similarities, now my angels concede a troubling truth about our children. Many of them become helplessly alienated from life's intended harmony. The curious innocence we admire so much sometimes gets tragically mutilated as our children grow and become poisoned by toxic leaders and teachers. Hate and prejudice are not inborn. They are not instinctive. They only exist because they are taught, or modeled after.

The evidence of this surrounds me days later as I'm forced to penetrate the smoke and dust of war-torn regions. What happened to the children whose sparkling eyes couldn't distinguish between the races or religions? Now they hurl grenades and launch rockets killing and maiming the same friends they would have loved to play with as kids. Dismembered limbs lay in blood-soaked streets. Homes and places of worship turn to piles of flesh and rubble. In split seconds, lives and families are destroyed. Individual and collective agonies last for decades, sometimes generations.

Many questions rise into the ether, mixed with the stench of death. Who on earth cannot see how wrong this is? Who can tell me what is so valuable that it is worth mutual destruction? What inner peace or great fortune is this mayhem supposed to bring us? How blind and desensitized have we become that we

accept such tragedy? What did or didn't we do for our young children while we had the responsibility and opportunity to mentor them, and teach them empathy and compassion? The angels are saddened and disappointed. It's clear that our work here is not done, they imply with heads hung low.

Our similarities are so much greater and more important than our differences. Yet some of us despise, or even kill one another because we feel so incredibly threatened by the differences in our chosen beliefs and faiths. These differences could and should be inconsequential, if we would only have the sense to 'agree to disagree' and respect each other's right to follow his or her own destiny. There are many good teachers who guide us toward many worthy destinations. So it is inconceivable that we will ever all march on the same path, or use the same navigational guides to steer us.

The subtle differences that make each of us unique provide valuable exercises in tolerance and empathy, if we would only recognize that opportunity. In the whole scheme of things should it really matter if Judy in Chicago believes in Christ, while Ming in Beijing believes in Buddha and Akbar in Kandahar worships Allah? If our religious convictions motivate us to share our spiritual side with a soul that is empty and searching for fulfillment, that is admirable. But, if in our arrogance and with lack of respect, we strive to invade and challenge a spiritually intact individual, then we are senselessly interfering with a worthy soul already on a worthy course.

Yes, there are many worthy courses in addition to the paths you and I have chosen. Christianity has provided a wonderful and important foundation for the society which I am a part of. And an arrogant

Christian may believe all who do not know Christ will suffer for eternity. Yet Christianity is neither the oldest religion in the world, nor does it boast the largest membership. Likewise, the tolerant Buddhist finds guidance and strength through the teachings of Buddha. Yet the arrogant Buddhist believes none will experience enlightenment except those who recognize the Four Noble Truths, and who follow the Eight-fold Path.

So, where will my soul rest or be punished after my death? Well, that also depends upon where I grew up, and which teacher I happened to listen to. My soul might rise into Heaven, or descend into Hell, or it might get stuck in Purgatory. It could wonder the gloomy underworld of Hades as Greek mythology suggests. Maybe I'll be judged in Amenthes according to Egyptian mythology. Or, could I be punished in Gehenna as my Jewish friend might explain to me? Then again, if I'm a Buddhist, my karma could send me to be reborn into a Naraka.

Any reasonable, thinking person knows 'all' of these stories can't be true at the same time. Yet each non-budging disciple holds onto his belief with equal passion. Heaven forbid (pun intended) we take a step back and try to draw some logical conclusions from these stories. All of the religions which these stories come from teach very important life lessons. And any one of them can be, and often is, used as a framework to build one's life around. That's a good thing! We make a dangerous mistake, though, when we feel we must discredit our neighbor's beliefs in order to validate our own. If we truly want to move toward a greater understanding of our spiritual potentiality, we will embrace, not shun, other religions. Each has its own very valuable jewels of wisdom to share, and those jewels should be

collected. By broadening our religious perspectives, and by expanding our source list of teachings and wisdom, we will surely be better equipped for this divine medley of creation we call life. We are serenely rewarded on our journey through life each time we discover a jewel of truth. We carry those jewels close to our heart because they help to illuminate the path ahead. The illumination allows us to avoid some of the pitfalls and obstacles.

growing into the cosmos

As infants, our personal needs are the only ones that matter. We are born totally selfish, which is necessary for our survival. We have no concern for the needs of others. The greatest lesson during childhood is realizing that those around us also have needs. We learn to share our mother and our toys with our siblings. As we grow into adulthood, those lessons continue, and we're forced to reconcile our own needs with the needs of our friends, our coworkers and other people with whom we associate. We learn to 'give and take' and to 'wait our turn'

and to compromise. Along the entire road of life we reach milestones that teach and remind us that we are only a small part of something which is much bigger and much more important than just 'me'. First there is common courtesy, then rules, then laws, all designed to respect and protect others who share this world with us. Most of us will become less selfish as we grow older. Hopefully we'll gain a greater sense of empathy. Possessions will mean less and friendships will mean more. The proverbial weathered wise man standing on the mountain top with his hands resting on his knotty walking stick has outgrown the desire for material possessions. Maybe we can't live like that wise man, but we can always try to see the bigger picture, and our role in it.

The big picture doesn't only refer to our relationship with other humans. Our role in this world is also intertwined with the animals that roam, the stones in the field, the tides in the oceans, the insects and microorganisms, and even the radio waves in deep space. Some cultures, such as the indigenous Indians of the Americas, understood this concept of interconnectedness more than others. Growing spiritually means stepping back, as our increased understanding permits, so we can see the world from a greater perspective. In essence, we are growing into the cosmos. The greater my field of vision, the smaller my obstacles and problems will appear. The greater my field of vision, the more appreciative I will become of each fascinating, little piece in the gigantic puzzle of life.

It's dark now. At day's end I carry with me a feeling of peace and tranquility as I paint the countryside with my cool and soothing brush. The stress and demands of the day have diminished for most folks, and now they engage with their families

and loved ones. The honest and affectionate interactions fill each other's needs just as the tide rises to its fullest potential under the smile of the moon. During these evening hours, the moon and I set the mood for lovers who embrace so tightly that I am unable to pass between them. My gentle breath and the moon's soft glow stir romantic notions in the hearts of those who are inclined to participate. Love is a fruit which grows on the tree of life. Without its consumption we will become malnourished and weak.

Love of family, friends and that special soul mate determine many of the little and big decisions we make. We've invested much of our spiritual wealth in these relationships, so we try to manage them lovingly and productively, sometimes selfishly and possessively. It's no wonder our world shakes when these relationships falter. We've entrusted those closest to us to carry some of our most personal and fragile belongings. In turn, we carry many of 'their' deepest thoughts and confessions. In love we become codependent and precariously vulnerable. We'll experience the highest highs and the lowest lows of our lifetime while on love's roller coaster. How we handle ourselves, and difficult situations when the roller coaster is at its lowest, will be a reflection of our maturity and self-esteem. Will we be able to step back and take a long, contemplative look from a broader perspective? Or will we use each other's trusts and weaknesses as weapons? Can we lick our wounds and search for the best path forward, the path which claims the fewest casualties? Or will we choose to retaliate by inflicting more wounds, exacerbating and perpetuating the painful exchange?

For all but the very strongest and wisest, it's easy to lose our sensibilities and let go of our controls during love's storms. My angels forgivingly attribute

our animalistic behaviors to our ancient fight-or-flight DNA. Those primeval instincts have not evolved quite as quickly as our expected social behavior. Sometimes the best we can do is recognize and compensate for those shortcomings by lending sincere consideration to the different options open to us. It isn't easy to devote our best-intended attention to our behavior while love's fury is tearing our heart out. But these moments do deserve careful calculation. What may appear as the best decision in the turmoil of the storm, may reveal itself as a hasty and costly mistake after the storm has rumbled away into the distance. Some damage may be irreversible, hence the caution.

My angels insist that every relationship, those that survive and those that fail, provide great opportunities for any student willing to learn. When we cease to be a student, then all that impacts us will have little value. My angelic instructors challenge me to become a lifelong student by placing this goal into my virtual pocket: To never end my spiritual journey, a journey that began with selfish infancy and now directs me through the lessons of life, toward my many awakening dreams - which will be found along the path ahead of me.

coming home

An orange thread lies on the horizon promising morning sun, and signaling one thousand angels that this journey is coming to a close. I will soon be returned to my pillow, but my essence has changed much since my departure. On the wings of angels, my insightful trek has heightened my awareness. So much of what surrounds me each day will now speak differently to me. My interactions will be mutually purposeful, and therefore more nourishing. There is no doubt that I have changed. So, too, did my future, the planet and the entire vast universe. It cannot be otherwise because all is intertwined, just as the entire jungle breathes with one pair of lungs.

Like planets and stars in outer space whose gravity affects other planets and stars billions of light years away, so every action we take has a perpetuating effect on everything around us. Science knows 'for every action there's a reaction'. That fact is inevitable because the amount of energy and mass in the universe stays the same, though it continuously changes form and direction as it reacts to its surroundings. When a stone is cast into the near side of a pond, the far side of the pond, and all in between, will experience the ripple effect.

When a bird eats a berry and drops that seed 20 miles away in an empty meadow, a tree grows. That tree becomes a sanctuary for countless life forms, and provides berries for other birds that come from near and far to nest there. More seeds drop and soon there is a forest. The landscape is changed forever because long ago one bird ate one berry. My angels encourage me to count the berries that were eaten by that one bird, and then to count the birds.

All actions, regardless of how small or insignificant they may appear, redirect the course of the future. The sea urchin on the ocean floor cannot wiggle one of its tentacles without eventually affecting a tiny finch on some tree branch thousands of miles away at some future point in time. My words of encouragement, or my words that wound, also set off a string of reactions. When the course of the stream is altered, however slightly, everything beyond that point will know a different universe. It is the unfolding web of life. In many aspects, the entire universe is one living organism. When we finally understand this we begin to understand our own divine importance. That importance discloses and displays itself during our journey, not at the arrival of some imagined destination as some would believe.

We are a part of the process while we live, and all that we are made of will continue to be a part of the never-ending process long after our limbs have been returned to the earth. As individuals we are a collection of all we have experienced from birth, and even before birth. Likewise, all of our words and actions become permanently woven into the foundational fabric of that which has yet to occur - that which is waiting to unfold - after we contribute our minutes, even seconds of influence. Each of us plays a crucial and imminent role in the evolution of the universe.

It is a great power.

It is a great responsibility.

It is an exciting adventure.

a collection of jewels

from an assortment of spiritual leaders

from a variety of cultures and times

Neither fire nor wind, birth nor death
can erase our good deeds.

♥

Holding onto anger is like grasping a hot coal
with the intent of throwing it at someone else,
but you are the one who gets burned.

♥

Religion is very simple. Religion is kindness.

♥

Treat the earth well: it was not given to you by
your parents, it was loaned to you by your children.
We do not inherit the Earth from our ancestors, we
borrow it from our children.

♥

Dig your well before you are thirsty.

♥

The Great Spirit is in all things, he is in the air we
breathe. The Great Spirit is our Father, but the Earth
is our Mother. She nourishes us. That which
we put into the ground she returns to us.

Three things cannot be long hidden;
the sun, the moon, and the truth.

♥

Joy is a net of love by which you can catch souls.

♥

We must protect the forests for our children,
grandchildren and children yet to be born.
We must protect the forests for those who
can't speak for themselves such as the
birds, animals, fish and trees.

♥

Faith is the substance of things hoped for,
the evidence of things not seen.

♥

There is no need for temples; no need for
complicated philosophy. Our own brain, our own
heart is our temple; the philosophy is kindness.

♥

God enters by a private door in every individual.

♥

We are spiritual people living in human bodies,
not human bodies with spirits.

♥

When we admire the wonders of a sunset
or the beauty of the moon, our souls expand
in the worship of the creator.

Just as a candle cannot burn without fire,
men cannot live without a spiritual life.

We are of the soil, whether it be the region of forests, plains, pueblos, or mesas. We fit into the landscape. For the hand that fashioned the continent also fashioned the man for his surroundings. We once grew as naturally as the wild sunflowers. We belonged just as the buffalo belonged.

Anger has no eyes.

They who give have all things;
they who withhold have nothing.

When a camel is at the foot of a mountain,
then judge of his height.

What is life? It is the flash of a firefly in the night. It is the breath of a buffalo in the wintertime. It is the little shadow which runs across the grass and loses itself in the sunset.

You are what you think,
having become what you thought.

www.ingramcontent.com/pod-product-compliance
Ingram Content Group UK Ltd.
Pitfield, Milton Keynes, MK11 3LW, UK
UKHW041928190726
13854UKWH00004B/1515

9 781435 744097